101 ways to get your adult children to

Move Out

(and make them think it was their idea)

Creative Outlet

101 ways to get your adult children to

Move Out

(and make them think it was their idea)

By Rich Melheim

101 Ways To Get Your Adult Children To Move Out
(and make them think it was their idea)

Creative Outlet
226 E. Myrtle Street
Stillwater, MN 55082
Phone (612) 430-0905
FAX: (612) 430-0907

ISBN: 0-9635106-0-5

Written & Illustrated by Rich Melheim

First Edition, First Printing

Printed in USA

To Emma & Duds, Jim & Bev
and all other frustrated parents who believe that
the end justifies the means

Table of Contents

Where To Begin

1. Start a toenail collection.

2. Grow and braid your nose hairs.

3. Have your gall stones made into a broach.

4. As a conversation piece, keep your recently removed appendix in a jar of formaldehyde on top of the television.

5. Tell them you can spit farther than they can.

6. Change the frequency on the garage door opener.

7. Blow your nose without a hanky.

8. Blow your nose with a hanky and use it to clean their glasses.

9. Recycle your toilet paper.

10. Wall paper their bedroom with "My Little Pony"

11. Join the Hell's Angels Auxiliary and volunteer your child to chair the "entertainment committee."

12. Iron a hole in every 6th shirt.

13. Practice the Mike Ditka method of public body-part readjustment.

14. Leave your toupee on the coat rack upon entering the house.

15. Develop a rare psychotic disorder that compels you to stand on one foot and yell 'Mel Torme lives' whenever they mention the word 'money'.

Weekly Subtle Hints

16. Weekly drop their checkbook into the toilet.

17. Weekly call them by their older brother's name.

18. Weekly back their car into the garage wall.

19. Weekly parcel post 1/3 of their laundry to Toledo.

20. Weekly ask them the consistency of their 'stool'. If they tell you, respond: "Boy, those were the good old days."

21. Break down in tears once a week lamenting the fact that almost all of your ancestors are dead.

22. Weekly wash their underwear, socks and all of their white shirts in hot water with a red sweater.

23. Use their computer each Saturday morning while eating a jelly roll , white-out all your mistakes on the screen, and accidently erase something marked 'hard disk'.

24. Invite the local religious cult to hold its weekly sing-along in your living room during *"Cheers"* reruns

Selective Recall

25. If female, forget to wear a bra. If male, start wearing one.

26. Volunteer to rotate your child's tires and, half-way through the process, remember you had a golf date.

27. Accidently forget a honey, tobasco & sardine sandwich in their brief case.

28. Accidently forget their clothes in the wash for the weekend.

29. Accidently forget where you put their car keys.

30. Accidently forget where you put their car.

31. Forget to take out the garbage.

32. Forget to buy groceries.

33. Forget to flush the toilet.

34. Forget to wear clothes around the house.

35. Late in the evening send them into the garage to find a wrench. Forget you sent them. Then go to the neighbors and call the police to report an intruder.

General Annoyances

36. Give their little dog a punk haircut.

37. Liberally apply the words "mod", "groovy" and "farm out" to your vocabulary.

38. Recreate the 'horse head' scene from *"The Godfather"* in their bed.

39. Ask "where are you going?" and "when will you be home?" whenever they leave the house.

40. Dress as your favorite 'All Star Wrestler' and surprise your child with a body slam from behind the door each night after work.

41. Regularly borrow your child's car, siphon the gas, smear Ben Gay on the manifold, leave a piece of limburger cheese in the glove box and retune the stereo selection buttons to southern evangelist and polka stations.

42. Replace all toothpaste with denture cream.

43. Replace all the liquor in your cabinet with prune juice.

44. As an anti-theft precaution, wood burn their initials onto every CD in their music collection.

Special Friends

45. Invite your child's 'special friend' for an elegant, romantic dinner and, half-way through the meal, remove and clean your dentures with a fork.

46. Regularly call their 'special friend' by a former 'special friend's' first name.

47. Blow up a few of those old 'baby bath' and 'bear skin rug' shots of your child and surprise that special friend with a 'cutie nudie' photo night.

48. Whenever their special friend rises from a chair, whip out a large can of disinfectant and quickly spray the seat.

49. Give a washed pair of lacy underwear to your child's special friend saying "Here, I think these are yours." When they tell you they aren't, simply reply: "Oh, I am sooooo embarrassed. They must belong to..." (turning to your child) "what's that other one's name again?"

50. Offer to show the video of your prostate surgery to their special friend.

51. Offer to show the scar.

52. Try some new recipes on their special friend: Like your child's rare, expensive, exotic fish on tapioca and waffles.

Evening Classics & TV Touches

53. Learn the fine art of watching ESPN, CNN, NBC, ABC, CBS and two scrambled movie channels simultaneously while controlling the remote.

54. Whenever a Democrat appears on TV, turn the mute button on and shout: "We wouldn't be in this mess today if Nixon were still in the White House!"

55. Trade in your big screen stereo TV for a 12 inch black and white model.

56. Ask them to tape "Hee Haw" reruns for you and edit out all the commercials.

57. Lock your TV on the weather channel.

58. Break down crying every night when a beer commercial comes on and mutter: "Zounds, child! Do you realize that none of this would be possible if free speech were not guaranteed by the Constitution?"

59. Whenever Bosnia, Somalia or crime in US cities are mentioned on the nightly news, turn off the TV and grumble: "I don't know why everyone gets so riled up about a bunch of dead communists."

60. Purchase a snoring tape and a huge stereo amp, place the speaker directly across the wall from their bed and, at 3 am nightly, blow the plaster off their wall.

61. At the stroke of midnight each full moon, enter their room buck naked with hunting knives chanting "redrum, redrum". ("Murder" backwards)

62. Sit at the bathroom window with a loaded shot gun each night to protect your family from alien body snatchers.

63. Tweak their cheek whenever they head to bed saying: "Oh, it's so nice to have you around the house, my little apple dumpling."

64. Sneak into their room nightly and drool on their face singing:

"I love you forever,
I'll like you for always..."

More Annoyances

65. Go on a diet and, in all seriousness, tell them that they must gain a pound for every pound you lose so as not to upset the equilibrium of the universe.

66. Whenever their private telephone rings, answer with: "My little pookey's answering service".

67. Sew plaid elbow patches on all of their good suits.

68. Rent the guest room across the hall to a Neanderthal.

69. Trade in the Lawn Monster X-KE 386 with bagger, mulcher and built-in wet bar for the push mower that grandpa used to use.

70. Try to squeeze a little tofu bean curd into every meal.

71. Plant 490 zucchini sprouts in Tupperware containers in the bath tub.

72. Invent 9 friends with infectious illnesses and repeat at least 12 times a night: "I wonder if that is what I have?"

Borderline Raunch

73. Learn how to toot "Old MacDonald."

74. Store your belly button lint in a Noxema jar in the kitchen

75. Grow penicillin in their underwear drawer.

76. Replumb the bathroom so that every time you flush the toilet, the water in the faucet turns just a tad yellow.

77. Practice knocking flies out of the air with boogers.

78. Lace all their favorite recipes with *Ex-Lax.*

79. Learn how to blow bubbles with saliva

80. Record your 'greatest belches of all time' and play them for your child's guests.

81. Subscribe to a 'learn proctology at home' correspondence course that requires a human guinea pig for lab work.

82. Stuff the fridge with your favorite dead animal parts.

83. Exhume Fido and perform an autopsy on the living room table to determine cause of death.

84. Describe your dear old friend Inman Hershinbecker's bowel resection in detail during supper.

85. Develop a neurosis about radon gas and place five day deoderant pads soaked in kerosene around the house to absorb the deadly gases. (You read about it in *'The Enquirer.'*)

86. From now until they move out, nightly ask: "Did I ever tell you about my dear old friend Inman Hershinbecker's bowel resection?"

If All Else Fails...

87. Give their name as a hot prospect to the Marines, the Jehovah's Witnesses and Amway.

88. Start telling 'knock knock' jokes.

89. Call your child's superiors at work to tell them that your little genius should be paid what she/he is worth.

90. Call their superiors back a day later and ask if the salary has been adjusted yet, or if you have to go higher up in the company to get results.

91. Ask to borrow money.

92. Buy this book.

93. Raise fly larvae on left-overs in the fridge.

94. Raise another batch of children.

95. Raze your house and move.

96. Raise llamas in the living room.

97. Take them on a two week bus tour to the Corn Palace in Mitchell, South Dakota.

98. Start a beginners banjo, bagpipe, & clarinet band.

99. Join the NRA, subscribe to the *Mercenary Journal*, and place a live cluster bomb on the end table as a conversation piece.

100. Talk often of your dear friend Tillie Bergine Smrzinski who never married and who, at 74, still lives at home to care for her 97 year old mother.

101. If you have tried all of these methods and still have nothing to show for it, ask nine or ten family friends to say to your child:

"You are becoming more and more like your parents every day."

Then start sneezing the word "rent" when ever they walk into the room. That ought to do it.

Good luck!

UNFINISHED BUSINESS

By Richard Alan Melheim

He parachuted into Kuwait. He slipped into Iraq.
He visited the Oval Office three times since the August 2 invasion at the
request of the president. Tonight he pushed his way into the apartment of
the ambassador who gave the 'green light' to Saddam Hussein.
That was his first mistake.
Maybe his last.

Did the U.S. lure Saddam Hussein into Kuwait as a pretext to remove his nuclear arsenal? Marine Captain Francis Khalil thinks so. The young American Arab caught up in the inner workings of the CIA's secret war against Iraq has stumbled upon information that is driving him toward a terrible secret: The war that began on August 2, 1990 may have actually begun much earlier. A winner wasn't determined until November 3, 1992. And it isn't over yet.

From the bowels of the Pentagon to the mountains of Kurdistan, from the halls of the Oval Office to the torture chambers of Kuwait City, and from Saddam Hussein's own bunker complex under siege to the apartment of Ambassador April Glaspie under lock and key, this novel compels its readers along an unnerving journey of suspense, deception and double-cross. In the end, this stirring work leaves its audience on the doorstep of some very dangerous questions.

"If Melheim's version of fiction touches anywhere near the public's per-
ception of a possible reality, this may become a dangerous little book."
-Grant McGinnis, CJOB Radio Winnepig

UNFINISHED BUSINESS, 240 pages, hardcover, $20 (Order on following page)

To order additional **autographed** copies of "Move Out" send a check, charge card number or your weight in bullion to:

Creative Outlet, 226 E. Myrtle, Stillwater, MN 55082
Phone: (612) 430-0905 or Fax (612) 430-0907

Your Name_____Street_____Apt #_____

City_____State_____Zip_____Phone(___) _____

Person(s) you'd like to have the book(s) autographed to:

Please send_____ copies of "Move Out" x $9.95 ($11.95 CAN) = _____

   *Minnesota residents add $.65 per copy (6.5%) = _____

Send_____copies of "Unfinished Business" x $20 ($23 CAN) = _____

   *Minnesota residents add $1.30 per copy (6.5%) = _____

Please add $2 shipping and handling per copy = _____

                        TOTAL = _____

☐ The check to Creative Outlet is enclosed
☐ Charge this to Mastercard Number _____Exp. Date_____
☐ Charge this to Visa Number _____Exp. Date_____
   Signature_____

(Inquire about discounts for multiple orders)